STITCHES OF A TORN HEART

POETRY

BY

SHUNAE D JOSEPH

ISBN 978-1-387-05147-2

CONTENTS

TO LOVE YOU IS TO HATE ME

To love you is to hate me
Don't treat me like they do because I'm giving my all to be here for just
you.
Don't insult my intelligence with temporary affections and or get me
misconstrued.
I don't run my mouth much but you'll miss this subtle touch
If at some point you feel neglect it's because my love you rejected
You may think you've fooled my conscious by stroking my weakness. Be
aware I'm far from weak let me show you the gift of meekness.
What I express to you is a pouring out of my love, positive vibes and
energy. A strong connection yet more wasted because your too scared to
see.
I'll sacrifice my will and strength to transfer to you because if you're the
true King that's what a Queen should do.
Despite your shortcomings I'll stay true to you but can expire. I'll be and
do the best that I can with all my heart so at least I know I tried without
future regrets when an ending transpires.
I'm in tune mind body and spirit a being cursed to see all truth even if I
try and close my eyes the universe still reveals it.
Once I realized you've challenged me to a game of chess I'm no easy
quitter I'll play just to pre-scope your tactics.

WHEN SORRY IS NOT ENOUGH
Can't take the deceit tired of the lies
When you manipulate my heart, you destruct my mind
My thoughts are scattered while you chill with good vibes.
You played me once twice or maybe three times
I say I'm done but then I'm telling myself lies
Can't answer your phone lets me know you're on some more shit
Don't call me right back, yeah, there you go with that bitch.
No, I'm not going to blow up your phone like I'm sweating your shit
I'm going to play shit cool and not going to even trip
I pray my next move is my best move
Checkmate and leave your ass like the last dude
Ready for this Queen to get passed you like hell yeah you in the past boo
Like fast food
Like bad news
I walk right passed your ass like
"Damn, do I know you?"
Now you've done wasted my time
I'm behind enemy lines
Fighting for a heart that was mine
When I get it back I open it to find that you drained out every ounce of
love inside
Filled it with empty words, wasted time, and lies
Makes me sad for the next because now this is all I have left to offer
It's fucked up it was my trust and love you altered
What happened to our dreams and wishes
Now you got me trying to mend my own heart with 16 stitches.

INCONSISTENT

I need people that'll stays real, consistent, won't neglect me, and are respectful in my life... but that's a lot to ask for... I know.

When you stop responding to people because you know they're unintentionally flaky and you prefer consistency especially that of a real friend

When you have to fall back from family and friends so they can live their lives and you not be a burden on them while trying to stay alive to live your own

When you literally flat out just stop talking because you don't trust people to stick around long enough anyway so what's the point of sharing your thoughts out loud so you shut down at the first signs of possible abandonment.

When you can't be loved because you're sick and people don't know how to help you.

When the hospital is so tired of seeing your face, they send you a letter basically saying just that

When your primary care doctor vanishes the entire practice so you have to start all over again after going through so much just to get them in the first place

When a judge won't even assign to your disability case to give you a court date

When you don't have sustainable income to live independently

When your good at doing many things, but can't keep a job because you'll end up getting even more sick

When you don't have a car to get your daughter back and forth to school, the doctor, or even a random day at the park or something

When you keep being put on the back burner for housing for you and your daughter because they don't think you can make it out on your own without help

When you were told you'd be lucky to reach 35 without proper treatment

When proper treatment doesn't work and so they take you off all your medicine to start chemo with a specialist

When the specialist won't return calls or messages to start chemo sooner and then automatically reschedules your appointments even further out leaving you shit out of luck

When your just flat out tired of all the bullshit but still can't do anything about it on your own.

What can I do at this point beside keep waiting and waiting?!?!?!

HAPPY FATHER'S DAY

to the man I hardly speak to because he's committed to keeping his vows
to a woman he's been trying to save and deny the truth
to you who I've inherited strong will and stubbornness. Our long talks
and discussions have ceased but oh how they are greatly missed
I'm jaded of call backs with twisted conversations and misinterpretations
starting drama only done from a jealous woman who would get so
discombobulated if she wasn't called mama.
to a father who sat by my side and cared for me when I was sick or
injured while denying the fact it was his wife who caused it. "What
happens in this house stays in this house" they say and when we have
company or go out, "shut your mouth", hid your scars, smile, and push to
keep all that shit in the closet.
to whom I'd have to innocently wait on the wall for until you get off work
so you could close out my punishment between 12 and 2AM each day.
I'm still just a child but before I could lay down I had to make daddy
proud and iron his work clothes for your 2nd job while I wonder "why
me?" but now thinking back, his wife had plenty time too those days.
to whom after all this time since the age of 4 after denying and
overlooking my claims and pains finally heard my cry for freedom at 11.
Who finally opened his ear to hear my story at 21 and apologized because
he was drowned by lies and deceit from her but the truth was then hard to
recognize.
to my father even to this day I can't fault you for trying to stay loyal and
true to your vow but I'm sorry for your loss because now you've lost your
child.

FALLEN CASTLE

There's more to me than what the eyes can see... I'm so broken inside
beyond belief.
The pieces of my heart now are as of the sand of the ground.
Many will attempt to remold my heart but just as your sand castles it to
will later crack and crumble apart.
I'm prepared to find Hope because with all honesty I feel my life is unfair.
How can you remain of good spirits once your house falls apart with
nothing left to spare?
The tears begin to fall because now I'm thinking over my losses and
failures.
My thoughts begin to scatter with doubts and insecurities that have yet to
end over this year. I remind myself what's done is done so what else is
there to fear?
I try and put myself back together and not be so selfish and turn my
thoughts back to you God... Thank you for still being here because
without you God this life would not be worth it.

FRAUDS

I'm sure it's some girls who are frauds but some of these guys will court
you by showing you who they want to be 'potential' or be all that you're
looking for and then later reveal who they really are.
Some girls will stick around and try to show them they'll accept him for
who he is now because they're thinking he'll reach the potential he
showed her at first... She thinks she has one up because she thinks she
know his heart and his potential... Most end up disappointed.
A man will change on his own accord and if he feels your worth it to him
then he will fulfill his potential or at least show you he is working to
change.

NO TOMORROW

There is no true tomorrow.
Today is now from sunrise to sunset they say.
Every sunrise is the beginning of today.
There is no time dilation to measure. Tomorrow is respectively the
beginning of today.
When you awake you say it's today…
not yesterday or tomorrow as those days will, within due time, change.
Today will remain regardless of time or solar pattern.
I press my hopes, dreams, ideas into today.
How can I help achieve or bring about a habitual drive toward my goals
TODAY...?
AS EACH DAY REMAINS…TODAY.
Guide yourself toward change today as tomorrow is only an excuse for
the lost efforts of TODAY.

BAD HABIT

You have a bad habit and I have one too
If we could just break them together maybe we can find our strength and
guiding truth.
We feel stuck and confined to temporary circumstances chasing time
But we can't see the road ahead because, our eyes, we divide.
Staying consistent for only a minute is not enough to say you are
ambitious.
Secrets, white lies and this system has our people set back with lack of
drive to beat the statistics but we all know our slack is being black but
why go to them to seek forgiveness.
It may be hard today but put down your tissues
Our days have been harder and or could be worse as we are born
survivors of time and today's worldly issues.
My people perish due to lack of knowledge and no it can't be obtained in
just school or college
That print out only prepares you for the system of e-commerce and global
economics.
Dig deep to find out the secrets of who YOU are
And when you find the knowledge you'll realize the answers were never
too far.
You have a bad habit and I have one too
Letting cynics bring our spirits down
Knowing damn well if we stay positively focused we'll get through this
too.

ACCOUNTABILITY

A lot of things happen in life that will try and break us down, divide our families, become destructive, or even provoke us to mock our God.
Ultimately this battle is NOT yours it's the Lord's
We are all accountable for our OWN actions whether provoked or not.
GOD IS IN CHARGE... HE brings conviction to the closed hearted the way HE chooses. Its then up to the closed hearted to REPENT and open their hearts and ears to hear the voice of the Lord for guidance.
All our LIVES are in HIS hands...
IF one has repented to the Lord as well as apologized and begged for YOUR forgiveness and you do NOT truly forgive them but pursue a destructive revenge... Should the Lord not do the same to you when you try to repent to Him and you have not forgiven the one who's hurt you and given them over to the Lord.
Our family needs fervent prayer to our God for forgiveness, the gift to forgive, and to help HEAL the deep wounds of our hearts, minds, and spirits.
Move us forward Lord and protect our minds from the tricks and schemes of the devil and provide us with the spirit of discernment to know the difference.

WE MET IN THE DARK

Depression is a mother****** and its hell to get through it. It suppresses
your being like your life is without meaning.
You lose interest in things you once couldn't wait to do before.
You hide yourself in that dark place hoping someone with night vision
and understanding would come looking for you through your door.
When you're in the world
you become invisible as the man with the sign "Money for food" at the
corner of the liquor store.
Your family and friends want to confide and depend on you for certain
things without understanding your limits and when you begin to open up
to express how you've really been you realize, before your first sentence is
complete, your words were wasted.
Obviously, your thoughts and dreams don't matter unless of course it's
about them or their own means for gain.
You wake up daily fighting with depression and pain trying to convince
yourself that you'll have a day with purpose all because God made you
worth it. You do your best for the day because you know your still here
and don't deserve to be.
When you opened your eyes, you feel confined as the day disseminates.
As the day transcends you get a moment of peace with a love that heals
but you push it away because you know it's short lived and will soon
disintegrate.
Love returned to my door and gradually pulled me from the floor. Little
does he know this is the final score.
Waiting for loves open door but instead there are walls that can't be torn
down but you and he only know that if he's the right one he'll do what it
takes and climb over them instead.
Awaiting a final chance to reclaim a life beautiful and plentiful. Where the
days don't slip by because it's a unique time that you provide that eases
anxiety and make any day worth living and more blissful.
The dark isn't so dark when you know you're not alone.
I'd like to break free into the light of day
Free to roam the world now without the glances and crooked smiles
because we're invisible anyway.
No one truly cared before being too scared of the dark and its uncertainty.

MY RED BLOOD CELLS

Your exactly what I need and you know it too. You make me shiver but
warm me up and comfort me with touches I never felt before or knew.
I want you forever to flow through my veins I'm praying for you too
I hope this fulfillment isn't vain.
I'm unsure if there's an adhesive for you so that you'll stay around and
really love me through and through like I really want you to. I just really
met you and already afraid to lose you.
I'm used to but greatly fear a repeated cycle of no real love, wasted time
and being deceived years at a time... They'll say the words just to gain trust
but I know the truth through their actions.
Most things start off great and blissful but that's the greatest time of
deception. When there's a painted canvas which isn't one's true
reflection... but with time that portrait begins to age, dry up and crack so
you begin to analyze and see it's imperfections...
those withheld truths you failed to express in the beginning now revealed.
Once you realize the paintings a fake... hmm well for me there's a hurt
damn near to no ending.
I want us to have time to really explore each other's exhibit without
missing a single stroke... I don't just want a painting of YOU... of course I
want you to tell me all about it too from there we then let each other
accept each other for who we really are.
I need your being to flow within me... help heal my body, heart and soul
with your sound mind and knowledge, your chasing faith and spirituality,
your caring nature, stern voice, soothing touch, stiffening grip, impeccable
kiss, arousing bite, steaming pressing closeness... I want your thoughts,
words, music and artwork to stain the glass of my brain so that I can see
you even in my sleep.
Be my oxygen.
Be my red blood cells.
Be what I need.
Be my King.
Be my friend.
Be my strength.
Be my true love.
Be just for me and I'll be more than the world for you.
Be MY BLESSING
BE MY RED BLOOD CELLS

I AM YOURS TRULY

I'm…

I'm your tangible calm through the storm.
I'm your covering through the cool night.
I'm your Sun through your shine.
I'm your moon when you glow.
I'm your breeze when it feels right.
I'm your towel when your wet.
I'm your thought when your quiet.
I'm your touch when your relaxed.
I'm your massage when you ache.
I'm your vision when you daydream.
I'm your pillow when you're tired.
I'm your tongue when it's sweet.
I'm your climax when it's deep.
I'm your heart when it's loved.
I'm your strengthen hug when your weak.
I'm your vibe when your lit.
I'm your kiss when you need me.
I am yours. Yes, I'm yours, so now you see.

…Yours Truly.

SWEET MEMORIES

I only want to create sweet memories. Let me later look back to treasure
and dwell on what used to be.
To say you were a part of me. A piece of life that's rare and that very few
get to see.
Tangible being more complex than the galaxy. My eyes surprised by your
beautiful perplexities.
Oh, how you inspire me. Coming out of this dark place to introduce me
to the true light you seek.
Blow my mind with soft kisses of knowledge and make love to me with
only the language you can speak.
My thoughts soon become yours as you take your time to get to know me.
Let me caress your heart, tug your soul, and ease your pains so you know
what's meant for the King to be.
Let's create sweet memories for we battle with time as it passes by like the
waves that come and go along our walk on this beach.
Seek the horizon no matter the weather
In due time things will be better because we support one another. I'll
cherish the memories we've shared together.
Maybe one day we could possibly say we made it last forever.

REWIND AND PAUSE

Those sweet memories you can't relive.
Just rewind, live in it a while, press pause, and soak it up all over again.
If we don't change we don't grow and if we don't grow we don't change
We all try hard to alter our minds of the present but once the present
becomes a memory we miss and long for it again.
REWIND
I long for you
like the sun that peeks between the shade tree branches
A sweet memory that never changes
Like your gentle kiss down the nape of my neck
Your lips stained my brain so I'll never forget.
PAUSE
…to be continued
…MAYBE.

DEBILITATING

I've pushed myself all week to do just the simple things people take for
granted
that they can do without much thought. This week was a GREAT week
despite 1 very
hard day and the rest better because I had support. If I feel as though I
feel better
than the day before I try to take full advantage right then and take the
opportunity do things I deem as necessary.

I'm still a mother and a wife at heart and though I cannot work with you
all in the work force I still have
plenty responsibilities to attend to. It's easy to assume that I lay around all
day chilling but
that's simply not the case. I'm usually resting to recover or preserve the
energy I have left to care
and tend to the needs for my daughter when she gets home from school
(McKenzie is ENERGY).
Pain invades me DAILY... a pain that one has to be built for... a pain that
supersedes imagining yourself
not only being hit by a train but also ran over by it without dying. This is
how my body feels once I've crashed...
I've overworked myself past my own limitations. Some nights like last
night I have massive trouble sleeping.
Imagine a large snake wrapping around your body from head to toe trying
to squeeze the life out of you...
You might pass out a few times from fighting the pain but you never die
and when you awaken the grip gets tighter
for about 2 hours before that snake gives up and you break free but your
left with the painful aftermath as well
but it's a little better than being trapped.

You have to get up and push through the pain because you got shit to do,
a life to live, and goals to reach
before the next crisis begins. Staying positive is a battle but if I don't do it
the train or snake going to finally
take me out. I'm too stubborn for that right now.

#Lupus and how it affects my Central Nervous System and Spine

CRACKED FOUNDATION

I've NEVER been truly happy trying to love in this corrupted twisted
world because
it's all for not when you're a reject of this country anyway.
When tragedy is brought to the forefront, it raises temporary emotions,
and then people
seek distractions to help cope (distractions to help you move past painful
issues blindly).
Our people give up hope, don't know what they can do, don't want to be
a target by actively
responding to it, and/or don't want to be caught in the crossfire.
I'd really love to know WHEN America was GREAT??
It's definitely a great force... A vicious tactful wolf and sheep's clothing
trying to save face
of all the lies and evil tactics to rid our people if we refuse to act or expose
this puppet show,
keeping a cap on population control and maintaining dominance.

This country's foundation was built on white supremacy... so when did
white supremacy end? When was
the foundation torn down and rebuilt? Prove it... Because I see a lot of
cracks and bandages
Don't be mad at our people because we want to stop being killed... We
out here begging not to be killed...
Stop shooting our innocent men, poisoning our food, pharmaceutically
destroying our bodies, economically
stressing our people to limited housing and government assistance to
poverty stricken communities
you've rejected, corrupting our children's education with lies and trying to
feed their subconscious with
subliminals and stereotypes etc. etc. etc.

The fact is though... Black Lives Matter Movement will ONLY matter and
make a difference to those of us who
are NOT apart or fallen agent to the white supremacists' culture this
country's very existence was founded on.

STOP WHITE SUPREMECY... So, BLACK LIVES can MATTER.

FAMILIAR STRANGER

When I first met you, I knew exactly who u were… You're a man of great
conscious and talent
a great friend and confidant.
I hate the fact that you've had to live out of your car and go through the
struggles of life.
You may not see it at times but you know the talents
and skills you have but soon you'll see that blessing the world with what
you possess will
have definitely been worth the wait.
I appreciate you being there for me during my struggles
and also allowing me to be taking this journey with u through yours.
Bless the world

BEAUTIFUL SNAKE

Don't stimulate my ego stimulate my mental
Evaluate yourself but keep it simple

Dissect your petty thoughts to discern the real truth
Don't think I'm buying your dream after all the shit I been through

My only time is for the grind and my patience is my fool proof
Puff heads or depredation is all you can seem to do

You in and out like diptera I should swat you with the plethora

You ask me which way is the grass I tell you go right you go left like
I was incompetent you come back pissed off because you lacked common
sense.

The grass isn't as green as you thought on the other side. I'm glad you
tried
because now I've rebuilt my fence so no more snakes can try to slither
inside.

KARMA

A love that developed too fast from all the pain and hurt of the past
The high you contained to chase but you failed to slow the pace
I try to slow down and not compete with time so I can find out if he's
really mine
I live like he is my King to only soon find out that I'm really not his
Queen
Hurting only myself with the thoughts knowing that from the beginning
my heart I should have blocked
To think that karma was bitch was a myth...
my karma is giving away my heart even after I see it won't fit.

OVERFLOW

When he pours his soul, it rains. Just what I need in these droughtful days.
I love the way he fills my pain
It overflows and washes it all away
I have the lock but you have the key
There's no greater love that my soul can meet
From day to night you just won't stay out my dreams
I swear you're the greater part of me.
Your better than my past that's why I'm so scared of you
Losing you I'm not sure what I would do
Moving on without you sounds impossible.

SOULMATES DEFERRED

The mere thought of you keeps my spirit high.
I'm connected to a deeper part of you that your very
being is unaware of.
Make room to meet me in the place our spirits
met before.
Uncloud your mind and judgment of all these
organized distractions you've chosen to block
me out with.
Don't be afraid to meet me again
I won't hurt or leave you astray.
Very few have seen this realm but overwhelmed and fearful
of the unknown, they too walked away.
The spirit of love is powerful, magical, and undermines all logic.
More astonishing than words of a prophet.
Let go of the world and connect with me.
Lose all fearful thoughts and hurts of the past and meet with
me again in that secret place that's deeply hidden
the place where you once allowed love to begin.
Feel me all over when you close your eyes.
Sense my being too every time you say "I".
As we have already become one a soul tie not to be easily undone.
When I speak to you I hardly acknowledge your flesh
I speak, write, and sing my thoughts to your soul.
You'll never claim mischief on my behalf. Only LOVE, HONOR,
COURTSHIP, and RESPECT
Our bodies circuit to a higher frequency when we touch
You can feel the charge replace the blood as it flows through our veins.
When I vaguely come across your mind I'm letting you know your
on my too.
But those moments you can't seem to get me out of your head
Don't hesitate to contact me because most likely my spirit
is calling on my behalf to you
because in some way I really need you even if it's just your presence, your
voice, your guidance, your love,
your scent, or your power.
I vow to love you always up until and even beyond my last hour.
I choose to passionately, deeply, and dangerously love you in secret, I'm
so afraid.
As friends is the destiny you've chosen but as the only one ready for our
forever to begin and I have to be strong to respect your wishes...
barricading my love and keep it, this secret.

STRENGTH

One of my greatest outside attributes
seeming as though I have everything together
or will have everything together
but my inner self is weak, lonely, and without much hope
my heart and self-confidence are completely
torn and scattered inside.

The strength that I had before came from HOPE and WISHFUL
THINKING
that soon I would be rescued and genuinely LOVED DEEPLY
and that all the scattered pieces would soon be gathered organized and
placed
in their rightful places and made whole again.

Why is it so hard to be strong and or even stay strong?

If I LOSE HOPE then I have NO STRENGTH, right?

I cry daily and my heart has been stretched, torn, and then scattered.
asking myself questions like
Where are you right now?
How will you survive this?
Will you survive this?
Who loves you?
Why are you so weak?
Why do you allow being taken advantage of?
Why are you so desperate for affection?

Strength!?, If you are real... come back to me.

YOU LOVE
but is this true

You love
but still do the opposite to make it true
You love
You love
but you leave me standing alone

You love
You love
but never home
You love
You love
but you show minimal efforts and speak half truths
You love
You love
and tell me you care
You love
You love
but still a blank wall I stare
You love
You love
as though you are here
You love
You love
but still you are there
You love
You love
but it's me you fear
You love
You love
but you're still searching place to place
You love
You love
but real love is in your face

You love
You love
but you're having a hard time to see
that once you've accepted this real love
you'll see many times you've already rejected me.

MIRACLE IN THE STORM

Dear Miracle in the storm

Don't be like me... be better. I am flawed with hidden truths and scars
unheard of.
I fight my very being daily even my own body hates me. I am not yet the
Queen I strive
to be even though I fight hopelessly to stand strong alone and deflect
from the pain you can't see.
I show you hope but not reality
I show you love but not reality
I show you joy but not reality
I show you hospitality but not reality
I show you a blinds eye
But why?
Why would I choose to show you half-truths and lies?
I betray your intellect, limit your mind's eye, and given you a veneer
blanket of protection
I fool myself with the thought that I am protecting you
But I'm harming you to not allowing you to see the truths of our reality
regardless if you're too
young to fully understand points of views and blocking your eyes from
the deadly truths of this world.
Some days I am ashamed that I played a part of putting you in a place
where we are hated and systemically
setup to be killed because I love you and wanted you here with me so bad.
I've been selfish
I've been selfish
I've been selfish
Trying to extinguish this burning desire to love beyond myself to run
away from this very reality that I don't
want to face or be in without realizing that the protection I can give has
an expiration and soon you too must face the harsh reality of this world
just the same